"YADA YADA YADA"

Published by OH!
20 Mortimer Street
London W1T 3JW

ISBN 978-1-91161-059-5

Editorial: Sheahan Arnott, Theresa Bebbington
Project manager: Russell Porter
Design: Andy Jones
Production: Rachel Burgess

A CIP catalogue for this book is available from the Library of Congress

Printed in China

10 9 8 7 6 5 4

"YADA YADA YADA"

THE LITTLE GUIDE TO
SEINFELD

CONTENTS

INTRODUCTION

When they met in the late 1970s, Jerry Seinfeld was the up-and-coming stand-up comedian with a big grin and clean, observational jokes, while the acerbic Larry David was famous for going on stage, looking at the audience, and walking off if he didn't like what he saw. But despite their apparent differences, they shared a love for discussing the minutiae of life and the gray areas in etiquette. And it's from this that Seinfeld was born.

Despite alienating audiences and NBC executives early, *Seinfeld* grew in popularity as the show went where so many others hadn't. It had people examining the mundanities of life. A whole episode was dedicated to waiting for a table in a restaurant. Another centered around masturbation, without ever mentioning it.

It introduced the world to regifters, double-dippers, mimbos, and a made-up holiday involving yelling at your family. WIth David's "no hugging, no learning" mantra looming large, the characters remained unchanged and unsympathetic, yet relatable, even as the situations grew more and more far-fetched.

Seinfeld has been off the air for more than twenty years, yet it still casts a huge shadow over the world of television. The adventures of a New York comedian, his struggling best friend, his outspoken, ahead-of-her-time ex-girlfriend, and his wacky neighbor still resonate, because, despite being known as "the show about nothing," *Seinfeld* was about everything.

CHAPTER

ONE

THE
BEHIND
THE
SCENES

While there was comedy on screen, there was drama backstage. Poor audience testing, crazy guest stars, a feud with Roseanne Barr and Tom Arnold, and multiple lawsuits all threatened to derail the show over the course of it's run.

"

Jerry: So, we go into NBC, we tell them we've got an idea for a show about nothing.

George: Exactly.

Jerry: They say, 'What's your show about?' I say, 'Nothing.'

George: There you go.

Jerry: I think you may have something there.

"

Jerry Seinfeld and *Larry David's* original pitch to NBC in 1988 reimagined and played out by their on-screen counterparts in "The Pitch" (S04 E03)

The Telegraph: *Top 20 Seinfeld Moments*

"

The pitch for the show, the real pitch, when Larry and I went to NBC in 1988, was we want to show how a comedian gets his material . . . The show about nothing was just a joke in an episode many years later, and Larry and I to this day are surprised that it caught on as a way that people describe the show, because to us it's the opposite of that.

"

Jerry Seinfeld clarifies that "the show about nothing" was very much about something during his Reddit "Ask Me Anything"

Reddit.com: *Jerry Seinfeld here. I will give you an answer.*

A lot of people don't understand that *Seinfeld* is a dark show. If you examine the premises, terrible things happen to people. They lose jobs; somebody breaks up with a stroke victim; somebody's told they need a nose job. That's my sensibility.

Larry David
on the unique brand of comedy he brought to the show

New York *magazine: City Slickers*

This is what the show should be—
this is the kind of dialogue that we
should do on the show.

Jerry Seinfeld

*to Larry David while the two discussed the
finer points of products in a Korean deli*

The New Yorker: Angry Middle-Aged Man

I think what goes on in people's lives is that most of their mind, most of the day, is occupied with tiny struggles. That's what people's lives are about.

Jerry Seinfeld
on why the show focused so much on the minutiae of everyday life

The Washington Post: *Jerry Seinfeld, a Stand-Up Kind of Guy*

"

Too New York, too Jewish.

"

Brandon Tartikoff,
then president of NBC, after watching the pilot episode of Seinfeld. Tartikoff himself was a Jewish man from New York.

TV Guide: *The Biz: The Research Memo That Almost Killed* Seinfeld

'You can't get too excited about going to the laundromat.'

'No segment of the audience was eager to watch the show again.'

'Jerry's loser friend, George, is not a forceful character.'

Quotes taken from an NBC research memo detailing audience feedback after watching the pilot episode

TV Guide: *The Biz: The Research Memo That Almost Killed Seinfeld, and* Pittsburgh Post-Gazette: *Jerry's gang is back: First three seasons of Seinfeld arrive on DVD*

66

I didn't care who was funny as long as somebody was funny and that the show was funny.

99

Jerry Seinfeld
*on why, despite playing a comedian
on his own TV show, he didn't mind being the
straight man*

Reddit.com: *Jerry Seinfeld here. I will give you an answer*

I had to look into the faces of those people, six inches away, so if you think Kramer is funny on TV, imagine his real face six inches from your nose, how funny that is.

Jerry Seinfeld
was much-maligned for his inability to keep a straight face at times, but who could blame him?

Reddit.com: *Jerry Seinfeld here. I will give you an answer*

"

I was written out of an episode,
I came back the next week,
and I said to Larry, 'Look, I get
it. But if you do that again,
do it permanently.'

"

Jason Alexander
*was displeased about George not appearing
in "The Pen" (S03 E03), and threatened to
quit and return to his stage career in New
York. George went on to appear in every
subsequent episode*

TheThings.com: *15 Little Details Even the Biggest Seinfeld
Fans Don't Know*

THE FACTS

In the pilot episode, "The Seinfeld Chronicles," Kramer is called "Kessler," because the person he was based on, Larry David's former neighbor Kenny Kramer, was unsure about letting the show use his name.

He eventually sold his "surnaming rights" to the show for $1,000.

Jerry twice calls Kramer "Kessler" in two episodes: "The Seinfeld Chronicles" (S01 E01) and "The Betrayal" (S09 E08).

I was in awe. It was like watching Baryshnikov choreograph a ballet. Every move, take, and line of dialogue—all the zaniness—was carefully constructed. And when the scene was finally shot, he moved effortlessly and brilliantly.

John O'Hurley

(J. Peterman) on the first time he saw Michael Richards prepare on set, and then perform

The National Post: *Michael Richards is the master of his domain on* Comedians In Cars Getting Coffee *(Robert Fulford)*

You gave me the role of my lifetime. That character would fit into any situation. There was a great universality to the soul of that character. I could have played Kramer for the rest of my life.

Michael Richards
to Jerry Seinfeld on Comedians in Cars Getting Coffee

The National Post: *Michael Richards is the master of his domain on* Comedians In Cars Getting Coffee *(Robert Fulford)*

"

George is bald. I am bald. George is stocky. I am stocky. George and I both went to Queens College with Jerry. George's high-school teacher nicknamed him 'Can't stand ya.' So did mine. George had a thing about bathrooms and parking spaces. So do I.

"

Jerry Seinfeld's
high-school classmate Michael Costanza unsuccessfully sued the show in 1999, claiming George had "damaged his reputation and caused him emotional distress."

ABC News: Seinfeld defeats Costanza lawsuit

He got fame through me! I made him famous!

Al Yeganah,
the real life "Soup Nazi" was another who was very unhappy with his on-screen portrayal, and let everyone know during an interview on CNN. When Jerry Seinfeld gave an insincere face-to-face apology, he reportedly screamed "no soup for you" and banned him from the store.

Neatorama: *The Real Life Soup Nazi*

❝

Up until the day of, there was a different ending and it wasn't that . . . [Larry David] wrote this thing and it was brilliant. We never rehearsed it because the audience was already there, we did it once for the cameras but the audience couldn't see it, then they pulled the curtain away and we did it one time in front of the audience. **❞**

Jason Alexander *on his famous monologue at the end of "The Marine Biologist" (S05 E14)*

News.com.au: Jason Alexander discusses his iconic "Marine Biologist" monologue

George pulling out the golf ball at the end of 'The Marine Biologist' episode. That's my *favorite* moment from the entire series.

Jerry Seinfeld
counts "The Marine Biologist" (S05 E14) among his favorite episodes

Eightieskids.com: 25 Things You Didn't Know About Seinfeld

THE FACTS

Elaine doesn't appear in the show's pilot episode. The main female role in the show is Claire, a waitress played by Lee Garlington.

NBC executive Warren Littlefield wanted a female lead who could exist outside the coffee shop, so Claire and Lee Garlington were replaced by Elaine and Julia Louis-Dreyfus. Claire's place of work, "Pete's Luncheonette" was also replaced by "Monk's."

Vulture.com: *The Lost Roles of Seinfeld*

I don't remember what the bet was. There must have been some money involved. I think it was a small amount. [The contest lasted] two days. Maybe three. I just remember it didn't last very long. I was surprised at how quickly it ended. I won handily.

Larry David on the inspiration for the show's quintessential episode—"The Contest" (S04 E11). The episode made David a contest winner again—this time the Emmy for "Outstanding Individual Achievement in Writing in a Comedy Series."

Vulture.com: *The Oral History of Seinfeld's "The Contest"*

For two weeks, that's how we started every kind of brainstorming session—listening to this girl's message. Then somebody said, 'We've got to do this as a story. We've gotta give it to George.'

Seinfeld writer **Spike Feresten** on the inspiration for George's "Believe It or Not" answering machine message. The writers allegedly left a message on the original machine telling the owner "watch Seinfeld tonight."

Fame10.com: Seinfeld: 10 Behind the Scenes Secrets

"

Lawrence Tierney scared the living crap out of all of us.

"

Jason Alexander on why
Elaine's father, Alton Benes, only appears in
one episode ("The Jacket" S02 E03).

Ranker.com: Dramatic Stories from Behind
The Scenes of Seinfeld

THE FACTS

While the cast and crew were impressed with Lawarence Tierney's performance as Elaine's father, he stole a butcher's knife from the set. When confronted by Jerry Seinfeld, Tierney claimed he was trying to make a joke and stabbed the knife at Jerry a la Norman Bates in *Psycho*.

Following this episode, Larry David would jokingly threaten to have Tierney back if the writers did their job poorly.

"

I think the biggest surprise to all of us was the staying power of Festivus. I think that completely surprised us. When I bump into any of the other writers, we're all shocked by that.

"

Not too many shows can say they've inspired an annual tradition on the scale of Festivus—something that still baffles **Jerry Seinfeld**

USA Today: *Jerry Seinfeld on what makes a classic* Seinfeld *episode: "Each has some insane thing in it."*

66

It was fucking weird, man. It did not have a set date . . . We never knew when it was going to happen until we got off the school bus and there were weird decorations around our house and weird French Sixties music playing. 99

*Festivus was based on a tradition started by Seinfeld writer **Dan O'Keefe**'s father to commemorate his first date with O'Keefe's mother. O'Keefe himself fought against the inclusion of Festivus in "The Strike" (S09 E10).*

MotherJones.com: Seinfeld *Writer Takes on Conservative Outrage Over Holiday Festivus Pole Protests*

66

People don't turn down money!
It's what separates us from the
animals.

99

*On-screen **Jerry** differed from his off-screen
counterpart, who turned down a reported
$5 million an episode to make a tenth season.*

Inews.co.uk: 64 of the funniest Seinfeld quotes to sum up
everyday life as the sitcom turns 30

"

Seinfeld reruns started prior to the *Seinfeld* finale . . . I got so involved watching that damn show that I never got over to my dad's.

"

Nancy Sinatra *on why she didn't visit her father, Frank, on May 14, 1998. The music legend died the same night "The Finale" (S09 E23/24) aired.*

The Herald-Journal: Seinfeld *spoiled last day with dad*

> **"**
>
> For the rest of our lives, when anybody thinks of one of us, they will think of the four of us, and I can't think of any people that I would rather have that be true of.
>
> **"**

__Jerry Seinfeld__ to Jason Alexander, Michael Richards, and Julia Louis-Dreyfus seconds before the four had to take the stage for the last time to film "The Finale" (S09 E23/24)

Variety: Seinfeld *Team Reflects on Series Finale on 20th Anniversary: "It Was Like the Last Day of School"*

"
No hugging. No learning.
"

Larry David's *mantra for the show*

The Atlantic: *Recognition Humor*

CHAPTER
TWO

THE JERRY, ELAINE, GEORGE, AND KRAMER

A comedian, his friend, his ex, and his neighbor. Four terrible human beings who don't even seem to like each other much, and at times don't appear capable of doing much more than making us laugh.

I do not know how, or under what circumstances the four of you found each other, but your callous indifference and utter disregard for everything that is good and decent has rocked the very foundation upon which our society is built.

Judge Art Vandelay
shortly before sending Jerry, Elaine, George, and Kramer to prison

The Week: *Why Seinfeld is still master of its domain*

"

I know Jerry. He's not a Nazi.
No. He's just *neat.*

"

*When Jerry and George are mistaken for neo-Nazis, **Elaine** jumps in to calm things down. Sort of.*

IGN: *The top 10* Seinfeld *episodes*

Just when I think you're the shallowest man I've ever met, you somehow manage to drain a little more out of the pool.

Elaine to Jerry

The Christian Science Monitor: *The End of Yada Yada Yada, But You Already Knew That*

It became very clear to me sitting out there today, that every decision I've ever made in my entire life has been wrong. My life is the opposite of everything I want it to be. Every instinct I have, in every walk of life, be it something to wear, something to eat . . . it's all been wrong!

George

reflecting on his life inspires him to do the opposite to everything he thought he should do, in an attempt to turn it around

Inews.co.uk: 64 of the funniest Seinfeld quotes to sum up everyday life as the sitcom turns 30

My name is George. I'm unemployed and I live with my parents.

George
does "the opposite" to what he would normally and lands a date with the beautiful Victoria.

Nerd Fitness: *Life Lessons Learned From George Costanza*

Alright, let's go deeper. Uh, what kind of man are you? Well, you're weak, spineless, a man of temptations, but what tempts you? You're a portly fellow, a bit long in the waistband. So what's your pleasure? Is it the salty snacks you crave? No no no no no, yours is a sweet tooth.

Kramer

unpicks George piece by piece in an attempt to work out his ATM code.

The Telegraph: *Best Seinfeld moments*

Hey believe me, baldness will catch on. When the aliens come, who do you think they're gonna relate to? Who do you think is going to be the first ones getting a tour of the ship?

George's hair was
playing the long game waiting for
extraterrestrial life.

Edinburgh News: *64 of the funniest ever quotes from Seinfeld*

I should be in a place like this. You get to wear slippers all day. Friends visit. They pity you. Pity is very underrated. I like it, it's good. Plus, they give you those word association tests. I love those.

George
on the upside of being institutionalised.

Edinburgh News: *64 of the funniest ever quotes from Seinfeld*

"

Jerry: No, no this woman is different, she's incredible. she's just like me. She talks like me, she acts like me. She even ordered cereal at a restaurant. We even have the same initials. Wait a minute, I just realized what's going on.

Kramer: What?

Jerry: Now I know what I've been looking for all these years . . . myself!

"

Jerry falls head over heels for Jeannie Steinman, a cereal lover with a similarly observational sense of humor after she saves his life

Boundless.org: Don't marry yourself

All of a sudden it hit me, I realized what the problem is: I can't be with someone like me. I hate myself! If anything, I need to get the exact opposite of me.

But Jerry quickly realizes falling in love with yourself is not all it's cracked up to be when your life revolves around cereal and the minutiae of daily life.

Inews.co.uk: 64 of the funniest Seinfeld quotes to sum up everyday life as the sitcom turns 30

"

George: I'm the bad boy . . . I've never been the bad boy.

Jerry: You've been the bad employee, the bad son, the bad friend . . .

George: Yes, yes . . .

Jerry: . . . the bad fiance, the bad dinner guest, the bad credit risk . . .

George: Okay, the point is made.

Jerry: The bad date, the bad sport, the bad citizen . . . The bad tipper!

"

George finds himself in unfamiliar territory after Elaine tells coworker Anna to stay away from him, but, as Jerry points out, he's good at being bad.

IMDB.com: Seinfeld (TV Series 1989-1998) Quotes

He's reliable. He's considerate.
He's like your exact opposite.

Elaine
*describes her new boyfriend, Kevin,
to Jerry*

The Cut: *A Guide to Elaine Benes's 29 Boyfriends
on Seinfeld*

❝

Dark and disturbed? His whole life revolves around Superman and cereal.

❞

*After George tells Jerry not to be funny around the woman he's dating, a more dark and moody **Jerry** draws her eye anyway*

Supermanhomepage.com: *Seinfeld's pal, Superman*

"

All my life I've been running away from that name. That's why I wouldn't tell anybody. But I've been thinking about it. All this time I'm trying not to be me. I'm afraid to face who I was. But I'm Cosmo, Jerry, I'm Cosmo Kramer, and that's who I'm going to be. From now on, I'm Cosmo!

"

*When George finds out Kramer's mysterious first name and tells Jerry and Elaine, **Kramer** decides to try a soft rebrand as "Cosmo"*

TVTropes.org: Who Names Their Kid "Dude"?

66

Elaine: You're extremely . . . careful . . . with money.

George: I'm cheap? You think I'm CHEAP? How could you say that to me? I can't believe this. How could you say that to me?

Elaine: You asked me to!

George: You should have lied!

99

When lying comes to you as easily as it does to George, it's easy to forget that not everyone is as natural as you are

Tvfanatic.com: *Elaine Benes quotes*

"

I can't stand kids. Adults think it's so wonderful how honest kids are. I don't need that kind of honesty. I'll take a deceptive adult over an honest kid any day.

"

George
*once again espouses the virtues
of lying*

Inews.co.uk: 64 of the funniest Seinfeld quotes to sum up
everyday life as the sitcom turns 30

66

Elaine: I hate people.
Jerry: They're the worst.

99

*The only question is whether
Jerry and Elaine are including each other in
this exchange*

Sportige: *Top 30 Greatest Seinfeld Quotes*

66

I love a good nap. Sometimes it's the only thing getting me out of bed in the morning.

99

George

show's just how important having something to look forward to each day is

Edinburgh News: *64 of the funniest ever quotes from* Seinfeld

You know, if you take everything I've accomplished in my entire life and condense it down into one day, it looks decent.

George
is not short of accomplishments, he's just spaced them out a little too much

ThePositivityBlog.com: George Costanza's Top 7
Words of Wisdom

Jerry, just remember—it's not a lie if you believe it.

George
distills his entire ethos down into one short sentence

Quotegeek.com: *Television Quotes:* Seinfeld

"

Assistant: My, he's sexual, athletic, an' without a trace of self-consciousness!

Calvin Klein: His buttocks are sublime!

"

Kramer
impresses Calvin Klein and his assistants while modeling underwear, after Kramer confronts them for stealing his beach-scented cologne idea

SeinfeldScripts.com: *The Pick*

> **"**
>
> Why do I always have the feeling that everybody's doing something better than me on Saturday afternoons?
>
> **"**

Jerry

was an early adopter when it came to FOMO

Edinburgh News: *64 of the funniest ever quotes from* Seinfeld

"

So I started to walk into the water. I won't lie to you boys, I was terrified! But I pressed on . . . and as I made my way past the breakers, a strange calm came over me. I don't know if it was divine intervention or the kinship of all living things, but I tell you, Jerry, at that moment— I was a marine biologist!

"

*Cometh the hour, cometh the Costanza. **George** relays the moment he was called into action to save a whale while out for a leisurely stroll on the beach with his girlfriend.*

Ranker.com: The Best George Costanza Quotes
in Seinfeld History

I'm a great quitter. It's one of the few things I do well. I come from a long line of quitters. My father was a quitter, my grandfather was a quitter. I was raised to give up.

George
on the Costanza lineage

Inews.co.uk: 64 of the funniest Seinfeld quotes to sum up everyday life as the sitcom turns 30

Is it possible that I'm not as attractive as I think I am?

Elaine

ponders why the man she's seeing turned down her advances

Inews.co.uk: 64 of the funniest Seinfeld quotes to sum up everyday life as the sitcom turns 30

"

Look away! I'm hideous!

"

Kramer

*sees his reflection in a toaster, and realizes
turning his apartment into a smokers' lounge
is catching up with him*

SocialMediaToday.com: *Look Away, I'm Hideous*

Food and sex, those are my two passions. It's only natural to combine them.

George

is a simple man, with simple tastes

Mustangnews.net: Whip cream, sex, and a cherry on top.

66

That's the true spirit of Christmas; people being helped by other people than me.

99

Jerry
at his most festive
The Telegraph: *30 great Christmas quotes*

"

I can't die with dignity. I have no dignity. I want to be the one person who doesn't die with dignity. I live my whole life in shame. Why should I die with dignity?

"

George
on how he'd like to go out

Inews.co.uk: *64 of the funniest* Seinfeld *quotes to sum up everyday life as the sitcom turns 30*

I gotta get some new friends.

Elaine

did get some new friends in "The Bizarro Jerry" (S08 E03), but soon found out she didn't mix well with nicer people

Tvfanatic.com: *Elaine Benes quotes*

CHAPTER
THREE

THE
DICTIONARY

Not since William Shakespeare
has popular culture had such an
impact on the English language,
and yada yada yada here are
some of the words
popularized by Seinfeld.

Anti-dentite

*(Noun): Someone who is
hostile toward, or prejudiced against dentists.*

First used: "The Yada Yada" (S8 E19)

Buffer zone

(Noun): Distance required between you and another person or people to make life comfortable.

First used: "The Shower Head" (S07 E16)

Close talker

(Noun): *Someone who stands too close to the person they're talking to.*

First used: "The Raincoats" (S05 E18/19)

Double-dip

(Verb): To dip, then bite, then dip again.

First used: "The Implant" (S4 E19)

Festivus

(Noun): A holiday for the rest of us featuring "The Airing of Grievances," "Feats of Strength," and an aluminum pole.

First used: "The Strike" (S09 E10)

Many Christmases ago, I went to buy a doll for my son. I reach for the last one they had—but so did another man. As I rained blows upon him, I realized there had to be another way! . . . But out of that, a new holiday was born. A Festivus for the rest of us.

Frank Costanza
explains the origin of Festivus to Kramer

The Telegraph: *Festivus for the rest of us: What would you like to complain about after 2016?*

Get out!

(Exclamation): A response to something unbelievable. Usually accompanied by a firm shove in the chest

First used: "The Apartment" (S02 E05)

Giddy up!

1. (Exclamation): Let's go.
2. (Exclamation): I agree with you.

First used: "The Baby Shower" (S02 E10)

Hard of smelling

(Adjective): Lacking in the olfactory department.

First used : "The Smelly Car" (S04 E21)

High talker

(Noun): A man with a high-pitched voice,
making it hard to distinguish from him a
woman when you can't see who's talking.

First used: "The Pledge Drive" (S06 E03)

In the vault

(Adjective): A closely guarded secret.

First used: "The Parking Space" (S03 E22)

Jimmy leg

(Noun): A leg or legs that twitch involuntarily when a person is asleep. Also jimmy arm.

First used: "The Money" (S08 E12)

Kavorka

(Noun): An intangible male allure. Latvian for "lure of the animal."

First used: "The Conversion" (S05 E11)

Long talker

(Noun): One who carries on a phone conversation far too long.

First used: "The Chinese Woman" (S06 E04)

Low talker

(Noun): One who speaks too quietly, causing others to mishear or agree to things they don't realize they have.

First used: "The Puffy Shirt" (S05 E02)

Man hands

1. *(Adjective): Manly hands, when on a woman.*
2. *(Noun): A name for a woman with man hands.*

First used: "The Bizarro Jerry" (S08 E03)

Manzier

(Noun): A male bra. Also known as "The Bro."

First used: "The Doorman" (S06 E18)

Master of (one's) Domain

(Noun): Able to resist the lure of one's own body and libido.

First used: "The Contest" (S04 E11)

Mimbo

(Noun): A male bimbo.

First used: "The Stall" (S05 E12)

Not that there's anything wrong with that!

(Phrase): Used when declaring that you're not gay, but you're OK with people who are.

First used: "The Outing" (S04 E17)

Pop in

1. *(Verb): To show up at someone's house unannounced.*
2. *(Noun): An occasion when someone has shown up unannounced*.

First used: "The Letter" (S03 E21)

Quone

(Verb): (Medical) Something you may do to a difficult patient.

First used: "The Stake Out" (S01 E02)

Regifter

(Noun): One who recycles a gift they've received as a gift for someone else.

First used: "The Label Maker" (S06 E12)

Sponge-worthy

(Adjective): A partner who is worth using hard-to-find contraception with.

First used: "The Sponge" (S07 E09)

Stop short

(Verb): To stop a vehicle abruptly with the aim of "accidentally" feeling the passenger's breast.

First used: "The Fusilli Jerry" (S06 E21)

These pretzels are making me thirsty

1. (Phrase): This snack is too salty.
2. (Phrase): Used to express one's general anger and frustration at the world, potentially due to being in a bar for a long time, unemployment, and a lackluster love life.

First used: "The Alternate Side" (S03 E11)

Two-face

(Noun): Someone who will look attractive one minute, and hideous the next, depending on the lighting.

First used: "The Strike" (S09 E10)

Urban sombrero

*(Noun): A large hat combining big-city style
with the spirit of old Mexico.*

First used: "The Check" (S08 E07)

Yada yada yada

(Adverb): And so on. Used to gloss over details in a story.

First used: "The Yada Yada" (S08 E19)

You're so good looking

(Phrase): Used after someone has sneezed. Much nicer than "God bless you."

First used: "The Good Samaritan" (S03 E20)

CHAPTER
FOUR

THE DATING

Over the show's 180-episode
run, Jerry, Elaine, George,
and Kramer date 158 different
people between them.
Dating and relationships are
constant, even if the characters
aren't great at it.

You know you could let the house go. You could let yourself go. A good-looking blind woman doesn't even know you're not good enough for her.

George
on why he'd prefer to date a blind person, rather than a deaf person

QuoteCatalog.com: Seinfeld, _Season 7, "The Wink"_

"

They call it a 'setup,' now.
I guess the blind people don't
like being associated with all
those losers.

"

Jerry
*doesn't hold high hopes for Elaine's
blind date*

Inews.co.uk: *64 of the funniest Seinfeld quotes to sum up
everyday life as the sitcom turns*

66

Sex, that's meaningless, I can understand that, but dinner; that's heavy. That's like an hour.

99

Jerry
on where he draws the line on intimacy

Everydaypower.com: *50 Seinfeld Quotes to Make You Giggle and Say "Ha"*

> **"**
> Divorce is very difficult. Especially on a kid. Of course, I'm the result of my parents having stayed together, so you never know.
> **"**

George

offers his perspective on his parents' relationship

Inews.co.uk: 64 of the funniest Seinfeld quotes to sum up everyday life as the sitcom turns 30

66

Elaine: You know what your problem is? Your standards are too high.
Jerry: I went out with you.
Elaine: That's because my standards are too low.

99

Elaine and Jerry explore the dynamic in their failed relationship

Tvfanatic.com: Elaine Benes quotes

"

Looking at cleavage is like looking at the sun. You don't stare at it, it's too risky. Ya get a sense of it and then you look away.

"

Jerry
schools George on the subtle art of looking at boobs

Twentytwowords.com: *40 of the best Seinfeld quotes fans still use today.*

"

George: Every time we go out to eat, the minute we're done eating she's running for the bathroom.
Elaine: And you're concerned?
George: Elaine, of course I'm concerned . . . I'm paying for those meals!

"

George

show's his typical caring side when he suspects his girlfriend might be bulimic

Babbletop.com: *10 George Costanza Quotes That Prove He Really Is "Lord of the Idiots"*

Salad! What was I thinking?
Women don't respect salad eaters.

Jerry
*immediately regrets his order when on
a date at a steakhouse*

Inews.co.uk: *64 of the funniest Seinfeld quotes to sum up
everyday life as the sitcom turns 30*

66

Why does everything have to be 'us'? Is there no 'me' left? Why can't there be some things just for me? Is that so selfish?

99

George
didn't take to coupled-up life with Susan—especially "what's yours is mine."

Scarymommy.com: 100+ Seinfeld Quotes That Are More Than Just "Yada Yada Yada"

"

Breaking up is like knocking over a Coke machine. You can't do it in one push. You gotta rock it back and forth a few times, and then it goes over.

"

Jerry

tells Elaine why he's sure she will get back together with Puddy after they bump into each other at Monk's

Luvze.com: Breaking Up is Like Knocking Over a Coke Machine

Elaine: When you're with a guy, and he tells you he has to get up early, what does that mean?
Jerry: It means he's lying.

Jerry
gives Elaine some insight into the male psyche after her boyfriend shunned her advances

Placetobenation.com: Seinfeld: *The PTBN Series Rewatch—"The Smelly Car" (S4, E22)*

"

How long do you have to wait for a guy to come out of a coma before you ask his ex-girlfriend out?

"

Jerry
asking the tough questions. If nothing else, Seinfeld is a show about dating etiquette.

The Southern Reporter: 64 of the funniest ever quotes from Seinfeld

"

Marriage? Family? They're prisons! Man-made prisons! You're doing time!

"

Kramer

tells Jerry why he shouldn't get married, despite making a pact with George that they'd both get engaged

ScreenRant: *10 Best Cosmo Kramer Quotes*

"

George: Why do they make the condom packets so hard to open?
Jerry: Probably to give the woman a chance to change her mind.

"

Given his struggles to open condom packets, George is probably lucky more women didn't change their mind

The Guardian: Jerry's all gold

"

To a woman, sex is like the garbage man. You just take for granted the fact that any time you put some trash out on the street, a guy in a jumpsuit's gonna come along and pick it up. But now, it's like a garbage strike. The bags are piling up in your head. The sidewalk is blocked. Nothing's getting through.

"

Jerry
explains to Elaine why not having sex with her boyfriend is making it harder for her to focus

Scottmckelvery.com: *The Art of the Metaphor, With 70 Seinfeldian Masterpieces*

"

You're giving me the 'It's not you, it's me' routine? I invented 'It's not you, it's me!' No one tells me it's them. If it's anybody, it's me!

"

*Most of the time it was **George**, so maybe he was just in unfamiliar territory*

The Undergraduate Times: A show about nothing? Seinfeld, 25 years on.

"

This whole sex thing is totally overrated. Now, the one thing you gotta be ready for is how the man changes into a completely different person five seconds after it's over. I mean, something happens to their personality. It's really quite astounding. It's like they committed a crime and they want to flee the scene before the police get there.

"

Elaine's
advice to Jerry's girlfriend Marla, the virgin

Top 10 Best: *Top 10 Best Elaine Benes Quotes*

> **Jerry:** What about the breathing? The panting? The moaning? The screaming?
> **Elaine:** Fake! Fake! Fake! Fake!

*Elaine breaks the news
to Jerry that she faked every orgasm when
they were together*

Vulture.com: *The 30 Best Elaine Moments on* Seinfeld

"

Elaine: Jerry, we need to have sex to save the friendship!
Jerry: Sex to SAVE the friendship? Well if we have to, we have to . . .

"

After Elaine tells Jerry that she'd faked orgasms while they were together, she realizes there's only one way for them to mend their relationship

Quotes.net: Seinfeld, *Season 5*

"

Elaine: I never knew you were so into breasts. I thought you were a leg man.

Jerry: A leg man? Why would I be a leg man? I don't need legs. I have legs.

"

Jerry

pulls no punches when clearing up Elaine's misconception

Placetobenation.com: Seinfeld: *The PTBN Series Rewatch—* "The Implant" (S4, E19)

"

Kramer: You know, things are going pretty well for me here. I met a girl.

Jerry: Kramer, she was murdered!

Kramer: Yeah, well I wasn't looking for a long-term relationship.

"

Kramer looks on the bright side of being an accused serial killer, after he is mistakenly arrested for murdering his girlfriend

Tvfanatic.com: *Popular Cosmo Kramer Quotes*

"

In my country, they speak of a man so virile, so potent, that to spend a night with such a man is to enter a world of such sensual delights most women dare not dream of. This man is known as the 'comedian.' You may tell jokes, Mr. Jerry *Seinfeld*, but you are no comedian.

"

*When Jerry is disappointed by the sex he is having with his gymnast girlfriend **Katya**, it turns out she's less than impressed with him, too*

IMDB.com: Seinfeld (TV Series 1989-1998): Elina Löwensohn: Katya

"

People on dates shouldn't even be allowed out in public.

"

Jerry
is not a fan of public displays of affection

Inews.co.uk: 64 of the funniest Seinfeld quotes to sum up
everyday life as the sitcom turns 30

I can't be with someone who doesn't break up nicely.
It's an important part of the relationship.

*When you break up with people
as much Jerry, Elaine, George, and Kramer,
it's no wonder **Elaine** feels this way*

ScreenRant: Seinfeld: 9 Best Elaine Benes Quotes

"

Ah, what's the point? When I like
them, they don't like me, when
they like me I don't like them.
Why can't I act with the ones
I like the way I do with the ones
I don't like?

"

George
*musing on one of life's most frustrating
conundrums*

ScreenRant: Seinfeld: *10 Funniest Quotes About Love*

"

Before this show happened, Larry talked about how MASH was about the horror and chaos of war. *Seinfeld*, Larry said, would be about the horror and chaos of being single in New York.

"

Elaine Pope,
one of the show's early writers, sheds light on the trademark cynicism and pettiness that separated the dating world in Seinfeld *from other shows of the era*

New York *magazine: City Slicker*

CHAPTER
FIVE

THE FRIENDS, FAMILY, AND FOES

Seinfeld's colorful cast of peripheral characters stole the show whenever they were on screen.

It was never really clear if the Costanzas were Jewish or Italian or what they were . . . When people asked me about this, I would simply say it was because we were a Jewish family in the witness protection program.

Jerry Stiller
(Frank Costanza) on his character's confusing heritage

PageSix.com: *Jerry Stiller confused by George Costanza's heritage on* Seinfeld

You have the chicken, the hen, and the rooster. The chicken goes with the hen . . . So who is having sex with the rooster?

Frak Costanza
trying to better understand farmyard animals during dinner with Susan's parents

Scarymommy.com: *100+ Seinfeld Quotes That Are More Than Just "Yada Yada Yada"*

"

George, we've had it with you.
Understand? We love you like
a son, but even parents
have limits.

"

When George's parents
have had enough of their son's lack of success
*in life, **Frank** breaks the news to George in*
typical fashion

Everydaypower.com: 50 Seinfeld quotes to make you
giggle and say "ha!"

66

Mr. Ross: I don't think there's any greater tragedy than when parents outlive their children.

George: Yes, I hope my parents die long before I do.

99

And, of course, George feels the same way about his parents, too

IMDB.com: *60 Hilarious Quotes from* Seinfeld

"

Susan: Hello?
Estelle: Congratulations!
Susan: I just want you to know that I love your son very much.
Estelle: Really? You do? May I ask why?

"

When George and Susan call to tell his parents they're getting married, George's mother is understandably confused

Quotes.net: Seinfeld, Season 7

"

I don't understand you . . . You have nothing better to do at three o'clock in the afternoon? I go out for a quart of milk; I come home, and find my son treating his body like it was an amusement park! . . . Too bad you can't do that for a living. You'd be very successful at it. You could sell out Madison Square Garden. Thousands of people could watch you! You could be a big star!

"

George's mother is suitably unimpressed after she finds that he is not master of his domain

Placetobenation.com: Seinfeld: *The PTBN Series Rewatch—*
"The Contest" (S4, E11)

"

He's in his own world when he hears that song. It's like I'm sitting there in the car, and . . . he's out riding fences.

"

Elaine's boyfriend Brett seems like a nice guy, other than his obsessions with furniture designer Carl Farbman, and the song "Desperado"

Rolling Stone: From Soup Nazis to Nuts: 100 Best Seinfeld Characters

66

Helen: Poor Marvin Kessler, he
went too early.
Jerry: He was 96 years old.
Morty: That had nothing to do with
it, the man was out of shape.
Helen: That's why we joined a
program. We walk once around
the block three times a week.
Morty: And every morning I eat
a plum.

99

Jerry's parents
try to embrace a healthier lifestyle after the
death of a friend

IMDB.com: Jerry Seinfeld as Jerry Seinfeld

"

Helen: Jerry we don't care much for the Costanzas.

Morty: We can't stand them.

Jerry: Really? Since when?

Helen: Since always. We've never liked them.

Jerry: Why?

Helen: Well they're so loud, they're always fighting, it's uncomfortable, you never notice?

"

*Maybe Jerry shouldn't
have been so shocked by his parents not
liking Frank and Estelle Costanza?*

SeinfeldScripts.com: *"The Raincoats Part 1"*

"

When you get to that chapter about my romantic escapades, feel free to toss yourself into the mix.

"

J. Peterman

was never one to let facts get in the way of a good story—even when that story is the autobiography you've outsourced to Elaine.

Uproxx.com: Let's Celebrate A Job . . . Done With
J. Peterman's Top Quotes on Seinfeld

I am shocked and chagrined! Mortified and stupefied . . . You know what these four people were? They were innocent bystanders. Now, you just think about that term. Innocent. Bystanders. Because that's exactly what they were. We know they were bystanders, nobody's disputing that. So how can a bystander be guilty? . . .

. . . No such thing. Have you ever heard of a guilty bystander? No, because you cannot be a bystander and be guilty. Bystanders are by definition, innocent. That is the nature of bystanding.

99

Jackie Chiles' opening address defending Jerry, Elaine, George, and Kramer in "The Finale" (S09 E23/24)

IMDB.com: Seinfeld: "The Finale"

"

They're real, and they're spectacular.

"

Sidra

removes any doubt from Jerry's mind about whether or not she's had breast implants

ScreenRant: Seinfeld: 10 Most Memorable Quotes from One-Off Characters

"

Why do they call it Ovaltine?
The mug is round. The jar is round.
They should call it 'Roundtine.'
That's gold, Jerry! Gold!

"

Kenny Bania

is easily impressed when Jerry helps him rewrite his jokes

KramersApartment.com: Kenny Bania—It's The Best Jerry! The Best!

66

Jerry: Leo, I saw you in Brentano's yesterday.

Leo: Why didn't ya say hello?

Jerry: Because you were too busy stealing a book.

Leo: You still say hello.

Jerry: Leo, I saw you steal.

Leo: Oh, they don't care. We all do it.

Jerry: Who, criminals? . . .

Leo: Senior citizens. No big deal.

Jerry: You could get arrested.

Leo: Arrested? Come on! I'm an old man. I'm confused! I thought I paid for it. What's my name? Will you take me home?

99

Criminal mastermind Uncle Leo gives Jerry a lesson in how to get away with it, although it doesn't appear to work for crimes of passion!

Flavourwire.com: "Jerry! Hello!": Some of Len Lesser's Best Lines as Uncle Leo

"

Jerry, it's Frank Costanza.
Mr. Steinbrenner's here. George is
dead. Call me back.

"

Frank

*short and to the point on Jerry's answering
machine. Frank was far more concerned with
the Yankees trading Jay Buhner than his son's
apparent demise*

Quotes.net: Seinfeld

66

Just let me ask you something.
Is it 'FebRUary' or 'FebUary'?
Because I prefer 'FebUary,' and
what is this 'ru'?

99

Steinbrenner
*might be more concerned with the minutiae of
life than any other character on the show*

QuoteCatalog.com: *TV quotes: Seinfeld: George
Steinbrenner*

"

Kruger: According to our latest quarterly thing, Kruger Industrial Smoothing is heading into the red . . . or the black . . . or, whatever the bad one is. Any thoughts?

George: Well, I know when I'm a little strapped, I sometimes drop off my rent check having 'forgotten' to sign it. That could buy us some time . . .

Kruger: Works for me. Good
thinking George.

99

*George uses his vast history
of dishonesty to help Mr. Kruger get creative
with his creative accounting*

KramersApartment.com: *Mr. Kruger—Not if You
Could See Our Books*

"

Joe: You know the story of
Pagliacci, Nedda?

Elaine: Uh . . . I'm Elaine!

Joe: He's a clown whose wife is
unfaithful to him.

Elaine: Oh.

Joe: Do you think I'm a clown,
Nedda?

Elaine: Do I think you're a clown?
No, not if it's bad to be a clown,
if its bad to be a clown then you
are definitely not a clown . . .

. . . But if it's good to be a clown then, you know, I would have to rethink the whole thing.

"

*Between a shrine to her
and his penchant for dressing as a clown,
Elaine has no idea what she's in for when
she starts dating the opera-loving madman,
Crazy Joe Davola*

KramersApartment.com: Crazy Joe Davola—I Like To
Encourage Intruders

THE ART OF LYING

The many appearances of Art Vandelay

"The Stake Out" (S01 E02): An importer/exporter Jerry and George say they're meeting for lunch.

"The Red Dot" (S03 E12): George names Vandelay as one of his favorite authors.

"The Boyfriend" (S03 E17): George tells the unemployment office he recently had an interview to be a latex salesman at Vandelay Industries.

"The Cadillac" (S07 E14/15): An importer/exporter Elaine claims to be dating to cover up George going on a date with Marissa Tomei.

"The Bizarro Jerry" (S08 E03): George tells a woman he is there to meet Art Vandelay.

"The Serenity Now" (S09 E03): George "sells" a computer to a Mr. Vandelay.

"The Puerto Rican Day" (S09 E20): George gives Art Vandelay as a false name.

"The Finale" (S09 E23/24): Judge Arthur Vandelay presides over the trial.

"

Newman: Let me ask you this. Don't you find it interesting that your friend had the foresight to purchase postal insurance for your stereo? I mean parcels are rarely damaged during shipping.
Jerry: Define 'rarely.'
Newman: Frequently.

"

*Jerry is unperturbed
when Newman tries to interrogate him about
potential mail fraud*

KramersApartment.com: Newman—When You Control the
Mail, You Control . . . Information

66

Newman: I don't work in the rain.
George: But you're a mailman!
   'Neither rain, nor sleet, nor
   snow . . . ' It's the first one!
Newman: I've never been much
   for creeds.

99

*When Newman breaks his
agreement to deliver calzones for George
and Steinbrenner to have for lunch, he shows
himself to be a dedicated public servant*

KramersApartment.com: Newman—When You Control the
Mail, You Control . . . Information

66

Newman: Hello, Jerry.
Jerry: Hello, Newman.

99

*This iconic exchange
happens 15 times across the series.
Variations on this include Jerry's mother saying
the line, and Jerry and Newman
saying "goodnight" to each other, dripping
with their usual disdain for each other.*

KramersApartment.com: Newman—When You Control the
Mail, You Control . . . Information

"

And I love that nobody ever asks 'Why didn't you like Newman?'

"

Jerry Seinfeld
on his on-screen nemesis

Mental Floss: *41 facts about* Seinfeld

66

Elaine: Oh. So, you're pretty religious?

Puddy: That's right.

Elaine: So is it a problem that I'm not really religious?

Puddy: Not for me.

Elaine: Why not?

Puddy: I'm not the one going to hell.

99

*Elaine and Puddy
were almost self-centered enough to
belong together*

Gothamist.com: *Mel Gibson, the Real David Puddy*

66

Serenity now, insanity later.

99

Lloyd Braun
gives George some advice, based on his time in a mental institution

Cleveland.com: *On the 30th anniversary of Seinfeld: 50 best Seinfeld episodes and quotes, ranked*

CHAPTER
SIX

THE
NOTHING

Exploring the
smallest-of-small details in
everyday life is what defined
Seinfeld right from the
first conversation between
Jerry and George in the
first episode.

❝

I can't spend the rest of my life coming into this stinking apartment every ten minutes to pore over the excruciating minutiae of every single daily event.

❞

***Elaine**, to Jerry, on why she's spending less time with him and more time with Kevin aka the Bizarro Jerry*

IMDB.com: "The Bizarro Jerry"

"

George: You're gonna over dry your laundry.
Jerry: You can't over dry.
George: Why not?
Jerry: Same reason you can't over wet.

"

Jerry's black-and-white view of doing the washing.

Inews.co.uk: 64 of the funniest Seinfeld quotes to sum up everyday life as the sitcom turns 30

> **"**
> What is this obsession people have with books? They put them in their houses—like they're trophies. What do you need it for after you read it?
> **"**

*Maybe **Jerry** would prefer the library, had he not stolen* Tropic of Cancer *in 1971?*

Inews.co.uk: 64 of the funniest Seinfeld quotes to sum up everyday life as the sitcom turns 30

66

Moles—freckles' ugly cousin

99

Kramer
on the hierarchy of bodily spots

Inews.co.uk: *64 of the funniest Seinfeld quotes to sum up
everyday life as the sitcom turns 30*

"

Jerry: I think Superman probably has a very good sense of humor.

George: I never heard him say anything really funny.

Jerry: It's common sense. He's got super strength, super speed; I'm sure he's got super humor.

George: Either you're born with a sense of humor or you're not. It's not going to change. Even if you go from the red sun of Krypton all the way to the yellow sun of the Earth.

"

Is the Man of Steel also a man of jokes?
Supermanhomepage.com: *Seinfeld's pal, Superman*

66

When you look annoyed
all the time, people think
you're busy.

99

George's "lifehack"
on how to avoid people asking you to do
more work

Puckermob: *28 Very Best* Seinfeld *One-Liners*

YADA YADA YADA

"

What could possess anyone to throw a party? I mean, to have a bunch of strangers treat your house like a hotel room.

"

*Despite constantly having
a house full of people helping themselves to
his stuff, **Jerry** is not a fan of entertaining*

Edinburgh News: *64 of the funniest ever quotes
from* Seinfeld

"

I love the name 'Isosceles.' If I had a kid, I would name him Isosceles. Isosceles Kramer.

"

Kramer

When your name is "Cosmo," there's probably room for an Isosceles in your family tree. It's no "Seven" or "Soda" though

Rugby Advertiser: 64 of the funniest ever quotes from Seinfeld

"

Let me ask you a question—if you named a kid Rasputin do you think that would have a negative effect on his life?

"

Jerry
questions Elaine on the power of nominative determinism

TVFanatic.com: Seinfeld

"

What evidence is there that cats are so smart, anyway? Huh? What do they do? Because they're clean? I am sorry. My Uncle Pete showers four times a day and he can't count to ten. So don't give me hygiene.

"

*Cleanliness may be next to Godliness, but not in **Elaine's** estimations*

Banbury Guardian: *64 of the funniest ever quotes from* Seinfeld

"

Kramer: What's today?
Newman: It's Thursday.
Kramer: Really? Feels like Tuesday.
Newman: Tuesday has no feel.
   Monday has a feel, Friday has a
   feel, Sunday has a feel.

"

*Who needs a calendar
when you can feel which day it is?*

Medium.com: *Tuesday has no feel*

66

George: Magellan? You like
    Magellan?

Jerry: Oh, yeah. My favorite
    explorer. Around the world.
    Come on. Who do you like?

George: I like de Soto.

Jerry: De Soto? What did he do?

George: Discovered the
    Mississippi.

Jerry: Oh, like they wouldn't have
    found that anyway.

99

*It doesn't get much more Seinfeld
than Jerry and George exploring explorers*

IMDB.com: Seinfeld: "The Boyfriend"

66

Kramer: It's a write off for them.
Jerry: How is it a write off?
Kramer: They just write it off.
Jerry: Write it off of what?
Kramer: They just write it off!
Jerry: You don't even know what a write off is, do you?
Kramer: No. Do you?
Jerry: No I don't!

99

Kramer tries to sell Jerry on committing mail fraud, but who's right about writing it off?

Forbes.com: Seinfeld's *10 enduring lessons about the IRS*

66

The thing about eating the black and white cookie, Elaine, is you want to get some black and some white in each bite. Nothing mixes better than vanilla and chocolate. And yet somehow racial harmony eludes us. If people would only look to the cookie all our problems would be solved.

99

Jerry

shares his own version of Ebony and Ivory with Elaine through the medium of baked goods

Quotecatalog.com: *Jerry Seinfeld (Jerry Seinfeld), Seinfeld, Season 5: "The Dinner Party"*

"

Oh, understudies are a very shifty bunch. The substitute teachers of the theater world.

"

Kramer

is suspicious of Jerry's girlfriend, Gennice, who is understudy to Bette Midler in the stage version of Rochelle, Rochelle

Banbury Guardian: *64 of the funniest ever quotes from Seinfeld*

"

I guarantee you that Moses was a picker. You wander through the desert for forty years with that dry air. You telling me you're not going to have occasion to clean house a little bit?

"

George

has a point. There is no "thou shalt not pick" among the ten commandments

Banbury Guardian: *64 of the funniest ever quotes from* Seinfeld

Hey, how come people don't have dip for dinner? Why is it only a snack, why can't it be a meal, you know? I don't understand stuff like that.

David Puddy
on what constitutes a meal. If soup isn't a meal, then dip sure isn't either.

Inews.co.uk: 64 of the funniest Seinfeld quotes to sum up everyday life as the sitcom turns 30

"

You know, I got a great idea for a cologne. 'The Beach.' You spray it on and you smell like you just came home from the beach.

"

*One of **Kramer's** many million-dollar ideas. This one was stolen by Calvin Klein.*

Banbury Guardian: 64 of the funniest ever quotes from Seinfeld

66

Jerry: Do you have my reservation?

Rental Car Agent: We have your reservation, we just ran out of cars.

Jerry: But the reservation keeps the car here. That's why you have the reservation.

Rental Car Agent: I think I know why we have reservations.

Jerry: I don't think you do . . .

. . . You see, you know how to *take* the reservation, you just don't know how to *hold* the reservation. And that's really the most important part of the reservation: the holding. Anybody can just take them.

"

When Jerry and Elaine are left without a rental car, Jerry struggles to comprehend how it happened

IMDB.com: Seinfeld: *"The Alternate Side" (1991)*

I will never understand the bathrooms in this country. Why is it that the doors on the stalls do not come all the way down to the floor?

George
might not often be right, but when he is, he is

Banbury Guardian: *64 of the funniest ever quotes from Seinfeld*

> 66
>
> Let me just finish my coffee, and then we'll go watch them cut the fat bastard up.
>
> 99

Perhaps the most callous line in the show. **Jerry** *to Kramer, before they go to watch a surgical procedure*

The Guardian: *How Seinfeld's funniest moments came to life*

66

Kramer: The bus is outta control. So I grab him by the collar, I take him out of the seat, I get behind the wheel, and now I'm driving the bus . . . Then the mugger, he comes to and he starts choking me. So I'm fighting him off with one hand and I kept driving the bus with the other, ya know. Then I managed to open up the door and I kicked him out the door, ya know, with my foot, ya know, at the next stop . . .

Jerry: You kept making all the stops?

Kramer: Well, people kept ringing the bell.

99

George and Jerry listen on in awe as Kramer tells them about his adventure taking his girlfriend's severed pinky toe to the hospital to be reattached

Quotegeek.com: *Television quotes* - Seinfeld

"

Jerry: See now to me that button is in the worst possible spot.

George: Really?

Jerry: Oh yeah. The second button is the key button. It literally makes or breaks the shirt. Look at it, it's too high. It's no-man's-land.

George: Haven't we had this conversation before?

"

Yes they had. Jerry picks holes in George's outfit in the penultimate scene in the show's history, echoing their first on screen interaction a decade earlier.

IMDB.com: Jason Alexander as George Costanza